D1672419

FEEL FREE TO QUOTE ME AGAIN

365 additional days of anecdotes, apostrophes, and antagonistic commentary.

The Captain

Always for Ashley.

JANUARY 1

Stop being so reasonable and take fucking risks. Move to a new city, switch careers, get a regrettable tattoo — just don't cut your own bangs.

If someone is throwing shade, they're doing you a favor. Use it to avoid sun damage — let your perfect skin be something else for them to hate.

Fidget spinners suck. If I wanted to watch something go in circles, I'd just start an argument on Facebook with someone I knew in high school.

Dogs make EVERYTHING better. Bad day? Pet a dog. Lonely? Get a dog. Ugly selfie? Snapchat dog filter — surprise, you're fucking cute again.

Remember, it could always be worse. There's someone going through the same shit you are, but with children, decaf coffee, and a cold sore.

The same guy invented both the bounce house and the fire escape air mat. Makes sense. Because life is either a party or a fucking disaster.

Maybe sharks just think we're all into kinky shit, like biting and underwater asphyxiation. Maybe they're just trying to show us a good time.

Makeup is cool, but so is intelligence.
Without a brain behind those brows,
you're basically just drawing a face on
a fucking volleyball.

If you need proof that most humans despise their own species, just watch the reactions when someone gets on a plane with a baby versus a puppy.

Feeling down because you only attract losers? Remember this: Truffles attract pigs, but that doesn't make them any fucking less exquisite.

Reading minds would be the absolute worst superpower ever. If you think people say stupid shit now, imagine what they actually hold back.

Dating feels like starving to death in a grocery store: There are plenty of options, but you'd rather fucking die because you're picky.

Don't be anyone's cup of tea, shot of whiskey, or drink-related anything. That's not flattering. Drinks are consumed and replaced with another.

If you see a girl with books in her purse, know this: She can beat your ass with her brain AND her books — a bag of books is fucking heavy.

Rejecting negativity is great, but I also do this thing called "rejecting stupidity." If that upsets you, you're part of what I'm rejecting.

Marriage is crazy. I can't even
commit to sharing my food with
somebody, let alone my fucking life.

How quickly a day can go from bad to good, and vice versa, proves you're always just one text, two words, or three drinks away from change.

The scariest ghosts in movies
are always elderly people or kids
because everyone's greatest fear is
either getting old or getting pregnant.

At night, when your mind won't stop, be grateful you have a mind smart enough to use protection — at least it's not a baby keeping you awake.

Don't follow the crowd if you actually
want to go somewhere in life,
because you know where the crowd
goes: Walmart. Fucking Walmart.

Be happy your friends get married. Each time, it's one less person to worry about canceling plans with because their life is basically over.

True adults make tough choices.
Waking up early, skipping a party,
having a glass instead of a bottle —
no fun, but you have shit to get done.

We see you trying to fool us with
your fancy-ass yoga pants and poses,
attempting to appear "balanced," but we
all know you're actually a fucking mess.

It's not enough to give her butterflies,
you need to also give her extra fries.
Because she might "like" you, but she
FUCKING LOVES carbs.

Don't let others ruin your day. It's YOUR fucking day. Work it, wing it, waste it — whatever you do — don't let somebody else wreck it.

Your goddess filter is cool, but you
can do other things with your phone.
Like call your mom to thank her for
dealing with your narcissism.

If Snoop Dogg can co-host a cooking show with Martha Stewart, you guys can stop thinking you're too gangster to help your girlfriend make dinner.

Approaching on a group of girls is
like approaching a pride of lions:
move slowly, bring food, and accept
the fact that you might fucking die.

Making dinner reservations is pretty cool. Aside from actually eating, planning to eat is definitely up there on the list of things I enjoy.

Admit it, you and your BFF are not peas in a pod, you're ice cubes in a glass: Trying to play it cool, but about due for a fucking meltdown.

If you're with the guy or girl of your dreams — and that person is not a dragon, mermaid, or dead celebrity — you have boring dreams, my friend.

Don't sell yourself short. Always get the long pour, the largest plate, and the highest of the high heels. Be tall, drunk, and happily fed.

Super Bowl ads are like first dates: Overhyped, expensive, and often confusing. However, the good ones always involve puppies or alcohol.

So, let me get this straight, you tell girls they're "basic," but all you do is smoke weed, buy sneakers, and play video games?

Dating is like taking a nap: It's risky.
There's a chance it'll be awesome, but
most likely, you'll end up feeling like shit.

The Sun's surface is 10,000 °F; the core is 27,000,000 °F. In other words, if you want the world to revolve around you, you need a brain hotter than your face.

Stylish girls are great girlfriends because they're comfortable being seen in public with things others wouldn't dare, like your goofy ass.

Sarcasm speaks when the truth goes unheard. Because, sometimes, being a smart-ass is the only way to effectively communicate with somebody you hate.

Have you met the one? First, ask
yourself, "Can I live without them?"
If "No," ask yourself if you're drunk —
because you're being fucking ridiculous.

Don't ask her to hang; ask her on a date. Hanging is fucking weak. It's for teenagers, bats, and guys who wear sandals in non-sand settings.

Making friends as an adult is cool
because you bond over mature things.
Like hating the same shit and wishing
you were drunk, dead, or in bed.

It's almost Valentine's Day; think your cat will get you something? Nope. Cats are fucking dicks. You should get a dog, or maybe a boyfriend.

You're not obligated to feel bad about anything. It doesn't mean you're heartless; it just means you're busy and "don't have time for this."

I want a girl who's easy-going, but also very passionate. Like, she loves taking naps, but if you wake her up, she might fucking kill you.

Roses are red; violets are blue.
Single on Valentine's Day?
More food and drinks for you.

What are scientists even doing? We don't need studies about poop particles on our phones — cure my allergies, find aliens, or go fucking home.

Think of your entire life like a threesome: If you choose the wrong people to share it with, the experience is going to fucking suck.

Be careful around girls with makeup skills. If she can hide a pimple, she can probably hide other annoying things, like your dead body.

Don't run from your problems, you barely finished the mile in gym class. No way you're escaping the runaway train of emotions you call life.

Girls, stop waiting for a man to sweep
you off your feet. If a guy has to trip
you to get your attention, he's a loser
and a fucking dick.

Imagine how pissed your dog must
be when your alarm goes off. It's your
crappy work schedule, not his. And,
HE WAS HAVING A GREAT DREAM.

You can say whatever the hell you
want when you talk to yourself — and
instead of being funny or clever —
you choose to give yourself anxiety.

Don't wait for someone to text you first. Dating is like sharing nachos: If you see a chip you want, fucking take it. Or somebody else will.

Hey, high school kids, don't stress over losing friends after graduation. The friends you have now will soon be the friends you mute on Facebook.

I want a girl with good grammar, but a sick mind. Like, her texts always have punctuation, but she's going to Hell for the stuff she says.

I bet Satan hates being compared to your ex all the time. He's probably down in Hell like, "What the fuck, Ashley? You're not even my type."

Stuck in a rut? Only you can pull yourself out and no longer be stagnant — relying on someone else to pull out will just get you pregnant.

Girl, are you a pomegranate?
Because you look delicious, but
inside, you're probably a fucking
mess that isn't worth the trouble.

Never sacrifice quality for convenience. Shitty friends, free tattoos, bad-yet-comfortable relationships — all easy. All not fucking worth it.

I want a girl who's intriguing, but also intimidating. Like, she looks like a girl I want to know, but also a girl who could break my nose.

Don't get carried away picturing a perfect life with your new crush, you should also picture them yelling at you while burning your clothes.

I'm starting to think that I no longer get hangovers and I'm just genuinely annoyed by mornings, microwave minutes, and most people.

When courting, male barn owls win
over females by bringing them food.
And that's why owls are wise birds:
They know girls just want to be fed.

Don't let labels and names change who you are. If someone calls a lion a pussy, that doesn't change the fact that the lion can totally fucking kill them.

Female black widows have the right idea: After sex, eat the evidence. No feelings, no cuddling, just a full belly and a good night's sleep.

What if we're wrong and being abducted
by aliens would actually be great?
Maybe they'll spoil you like a pet Golden
Retriever or something.

Surprisingly, girls with cats make the best girlfriends. Because they've learned to love something selfish and dumb — like your childish ass.

A girl owns one cat per personality. A single cat? Kind of normal. Two cats? Weird, but what girl isn't? Three or more? Fucking run, dude.

Daylight Saving Time shows us
the value of a single hour; yet,
here you are, about to waste three
of them watching the finale of
some reality show.

Don't complain about losing an hour with Daylight Saving Time. I lose at least two hours every weekend from blackout drinking — it's not that bad.

I want a girl with a savvy sense of fashion, but a sick sense of humor. Like, if you think her outfits are crazy, just wait for what comes out of her mouth.

Approach dating new people the same way you approach spiders: Keep your distance, move slowly, and fucking smash them if they try to hurt you.

Don't fear change; it's good for you. Unless it involves sobriety, going to prison, or not eating dairy — those changes sound fucking awful.

Instead of comparing yourself to
perfect people you see online,
compare yourself to people you see at
airports losing their fucking minds.

Don't bring your bed pillow to the airport. You look like a grumpy, upset child who just called their mom to come get them from a sleepover.

Remember, St. Patrick was just that: a saint. So do your best to pretend you're not going to Hell for half of the things you'll do or say tonight.

Instead of arguing with strangers
on social media, consider getting a
fucking job so you have less free time
to spend embarrassing yourself.

I want a girl who's carefree, but also cutthroat. Like, she does peaceful shit like meditate, but if necessary, she can absolutely regulate.

You won't find inspiration within your hesitation. To live an interesting life: take risks, say "Fuck this," and don't ever let yourself be useless.

Maybe you're not in love. Maybe you're just tired, thinking irrationally. Like when your alarm goes off and you'd do ANYTHING to stay in bed.

The modern-day "Romeo and Juliet" would just be a girl named Julie who ignores everyone's advice and always goes back to her douchey ex, Rob.

I'm not so sure humans top the
animal kingdom. As far as I know,
we're the only species lame enough
to use a "U up?" text as a mating call.

On Fridays, if you're a lightweight, just stay home; embarrass yourself in front of your pets instead of actual people.

There's nothing wrong with not being liked. Some people don't like dogs — obviously, those people are dumb — but dogs don't let it bother them.

I don't trust people who "meal prep." Anyone with a fridge full of pre-planned meals, probably has a freezer full of human body parts.

Enjoy being single: Be selfish with your time, money, and space. Cancel plans. Buy shit you don't need. Sleep like a fucking starfish.

You can delete a post, but you can't erase a memory. We all know that "can't wait to spend the rest of our lives together" caption happened.

Guys, be polite. If you ask her to
hold things in her purse for you,
return the favor: hold the door, her
hand, and her hair if she pukes.

Don't be "the one that got away," be
the one who will make them someday
say, "Holy fuck, we used to date" —
and nobody will believe them.

At night, if you're having trouble falling asleep, just go look at how boring your married friends' Instagram accounts are.

I support male rompers. Any guy can walk a mile in his girlfriend's shoes, but a real man will do it with a wedgie while trying not to piss himself.

Nothing in life I'd rather do than raise a daughter who's a fucking badass. Aside from not having kids at all, obviously. But, IF I DID . . .

Holding a grudge for years is like leaving a cast on a broken leg long after it's healed: Why are you limping through life for no fucking reason?

Blind dates are good for you because
they get you out of your comfort zone.
AND remind you that other people
often don't know what's right for you.

Dating apps are like going to a zoo:
It's fun to look at different creatures,
but meeting some of them up close
would be fucking terrifying.

Birds literally just eat, travel, and shit on things they don't like. I don't know about you, but that's the lifestyle I'm striving for.

If by "sleep like a baby" you mean
wake up in the middle of the night
demanding food and attention, then,
yeah, she does that quite often.

Apparently, "Nice guys finish last."
Well, there's your problem, ladies, your
boyfriend sucks at sex because you're
dating a fucking jerk.

Take him to the animal shelter on your
first date; show him his competition.
Sure, he's tall, but look at the cute,
little tail on that guy.

If you want to test your relationship, actually test them: Give the other person a midterm every six weeks to see if they've paid attention.

I want a girl who's unpredictable, but always prepared. Like, her life is full of mystery, and her purse, well, that's just full of snacks.

Dating is a staircase, full of missteps, slips, and embarrassing moments. So, dress well; at least look good falling down that staircase.

The next time you're feeling dumb,
just think, somewhere out there
is a girl forgiving her boyfriend for
cheating on her for the fifth time.

Revenge is NOT a dish best served cold. It's a dish best served as a series of great outfits, bomb selfies, and cryptic social media posts.

The Tinder icon is a fireball in order to represent the fact that your dating life must feel like fucking Hell if you've resorted to using Tinder.

Don't underestimate her. She might
not be able to draw a self-portrait
to save her life, but she can draw
conclusions to justify ending yours.

I want a girl who's weird, but also feared. Like, she's really goofy, but nobody dares to make fun of her because she's also a fucking boss.

I've spent a lot of money on alcohol and a lot of time around people I didn't like; I've chosen to save my sanity instead of save my money.

Girls always wear socks because their feet are always cold . . . Like their hands, and their hearts.

As a kid, it only mattered whether or
not the person you liked had cooties.
Now, do they have a kid, an STD, a job,
a cat, a drug problem . . .

You can apologize, you can pretend it didn't happen, but all trust is broken the moment somebody notices their leftovers have been eaten.

Guys, if a girl asks about your zodiac sign, just play along. Because chances are you have dating criteria that's equally as fucking dumb.

"I'm open-minded, free-spirited, and independent," says the individual who uses zodiac signs as an immediate form of judgment.

Girls, if a man says to you, "Women belong in the kitchen," you belong in a car — running his ass over for being an ignorant piece of shit.

When you finish binge watching a Netflix series, don't get bummed out. At least it lasted longer than your last relationship.

SUMMER PREP: Buy juice. Pour it out.
Refill with alcohol of choice. Drink.
Repeat until you no longer care about
your fucking juice cleanse.

Monday is like your face: You can hate it, you can complain about it, but guess what? It's not going anywhere — so learn to like it.

The next time you read a stupid online comment, remind yourself, these are the same people you entrust with your life every time you drive.

I want a girl who's punctual, but unpredictable. Like, she's always on time for a date, but she might arrive dressed like a fucking vampire.

Dudes, if a girl answers your text with "K," immediately stop what you're doing. Respect the rules of the "safe word" and nobody gets hurt.

Dating is like walking into traffic: Be smart. If you ignore signals in order to "follow your heart," prepare to get hit by a fucking car.

Stop saying you're "accepting applications" for people to date you. I'm sorry, but if dating you is a job, nobody wants that position.

It's okay to burn bridges; it forces you to find a new way. Sure, it might take you longer, but don't act like you couldn't use the cardio.

Look at you. You survived another
Monday. You should probably add
that shit to your resume and go get
a job you actually like.

If somebody is trying to send you on a guilt trip, make them buy you a few drinks first — treat that trip like a vacation and just get wasted.

Dating is like getting a really bad sunburn: At first, it feels good to go out, but eventually you regret ever leaving your house.

It's good to have a Saturday routine;
especially when that routine
involves weird texts, waffles,
and waking up still drunk.

Breaking up would be so easy if dinosaurs were still alive. You'd just go camping and wait for a T-Rex to eat the other person.

Stop saying you're going to own "like 23 dogs" — that's just irresponsible. You can barely take care of yourself.

It's nice to be attractive, but more importantly, be proactive. Be someone who makes shit happen, not one who relies on others to notice them.

Stop making excuses for not reaching your goals. Oscar the Grouch lives in a fucking trashcan AND STILL has a successful television career.

Dating is a never-ending game of Duck, Duck, Goose: Ignore most people, find one you like, then run away because you're afraid of commitment.

I want a girl who's decisive and impulsive. Like, she knows exactly where she wants to eat, but the idea of her with a steak knife is fucking sketchy.

If you love someone, set them free.
Or, just set unrealistic expectations
about text message responsiveness
until they leave on their own.

During the 1800s, hair was a romantic gift. Basically, your girlfriend leaves hair everywhere because she fucking loves you, you dumb idiot.

It's called the dating pool because
it's like a public swimming pool:
Full of shit, but getting in seems
like a good idea when you're drunk.

So you don't like "adulting," but you want to spend all summer taking photos on a boat? Huh, you know who owns a boat? Somebody who's adulting.

That's cool you spent $30 on a bottle
of hairspray, but it's too bad it only
helps you control frizz and not the
real problems in your life.

Dating spelled backwards is "gnitad."
It's confusing and makes no fucking
sense, kind of like your dating life.

Werewolves are like that friend who
only comes out once a month, over
does it, loses their fucking clothes,
and doesn't remember anything.

Oh, you're drowning in emotions?
That's too bad. Maybe you should
consider drowning the friend who let
you leave the house in that dress.

Dating is like taking a shower: It's a hassle, but it's necessary. Because, if you refuse to do it, you'll probably never get laid.

Life's short, but not so short you
should freak out. Relax, you'll find
someone else. You'll get a new job.
You'll see another dog tomorrow.

Parents who publicly shame their
kids are losers. We get it: You're
trying to get the attention you didn't
receive when you were a kid.

I want a girl with a strong personality, but even stronger thighs. Like, she can easily get inside my head, but also choke me out in bed.

Going to a bar on a budget is like going to a buffet on a diet: Just give up and accept the fact that you'll probably hate yourself tomorrow.

Instead of worrying about getting a text back, worry about getting your life on track. Go chase some fucking goals instead of chasing ass.

Don't lie to a girl who can write cursive;
she'll connect the dots as easily as a 'q' to
a 'u.' In other words, good luck, buddy —
you're dating a detective.

Instagram needs flame graphics
when you delete a photo, giving you
the feeling of lighting your ex on fire,
without involving the police.

Girls love two things: telling lies and eating in bed. If she acts gluten-free in the streets, trust me, she's a pizza fiend in the sheets.

Stop living your life like everyone else or you'll be just another pigeon in the flock. Fly solo, like an eagle, or a scary fucking hawk.

I once saw a dude wearing a puffy coat, cargo shorts, and yellow shoes. Women, WE NEED YOU. Your boyfriend can't even fucking dress himself.

She's not too picky, she just knows she has options. Ever seen a makeup aisle? There are 37 shades of blue; dating works the same way, dude.

Girls with cracked phones make the best girlfriends. Because they've learned to deal with something annoying, like your dumb, immature ass.

It's Friday, meaning you have roughly 48 hours to reward yourself for making it through five days without killing yourself or somebody else.

Children are not the future, robots are.
When is the last time you saw a kid drive
a car without crashing it?

Stop blaming other people for the way your life is. You know who does that? Kids. You know what else kids do? Live with their parents.

Your life is like a chainsaw: If you remain motionless, you serve no purpose. So get up, get moving, and cut off today's dick.

We need to call it something other than "ghosting." Why? Because ghosts don't leave, they hang around. THAT'S WHY HOUSES ARE FUCKING HAUNTED.

Imagine if people cared about actual
wars as much as they do Star Wars.

Sure, you don't use algebra often, but you did learn to cope with confusion, frustration, and despair. So at least you're ready for dating.

Breakfast is not the most important meal of the day. The most important meal is the one you have to eat to avoid getting too drunk too early.

Your girlfriend cries when she's
happy because she knows,
in about five minutes, you're
probably going to say something
dumb that will fuck it all up.

Building a relationship is like building a house: It doesn't matter how good it looks on the outside if the foundation is fucking shit.

"Afraid of getting hurt" isn't an excuse to be single; it's an excuse to not own a motorcycle. Oddly enough, owning a motorcycle might help you get a girlfriend.

I'm hard to date because I'm like a hunting dog. I'm loyal and you can pet me, but I'm happiest when I'm running around trying to kill shit.

Never put me on speakerphone. If I
wanted everybody to know my business,
I'd post something on Facebook that's
both cryptic and ridiculous.

I'm not sure why everyone is so afraid of clowns, but it's nice to see society come together to combat unblended contour and overdrawn lips.

If you go out, wear all black and pass out with your clothes on. When you wake up, you'll already be dressed to mourn the loss of your dignity.

Everyone these days is so afraid of
commitment that the scariest thing is
no longer being attacked by a shark,
it's being asked out on a date by one.

I want a girl who's reliable, but also ravenous. Like, she can definitely keep a secret, but also crush an entire box of Cheez-Its.

It would make more sense if the forbidden fruit in The Bible were from an avocado tree. Of course Eve couldn't resist it — everybody loves guacamole.

Time is valuable. Don't be childish and waste someone's time if it's not going anywhere. Waste your own time, you know, like you did your childhood.

Date like you order food at a restaurant: Be selective, ask questions, and if it's garbage, don't even think about bringing it home.

Everybody has a deal-breaker; some just haven't found it. They're not desperate — they just don't know how fucking awful some people are yet.

Coloring book dates should be a thing. How someone colors an apple definitely reveals their personality: sweet, sour, or fucking poisonous?

Bad relationships are like leftovers: When they go bad, you'll make yourself sick if you insist on saving them — throw that shit in the trash and start over.

An anxious life is an open book, but kind of like one of those "Choose Your Own Adventure" books where everything is a life-or-death decision.

Happiness is a choice. For example:
You can CHOOSE to eat a salad and be
fucking miserable, or you can order a
burrito and live your life.

Plagiarism is like telling everyone
you "hooked up" when all you did was
cuddle: Eventually, the truth comes out
and you look like an idiot.

As a society, we're obsessed with things that aren't real — like unicorns, fake boobs, and the possibility of "just one drink."

"Friends with benefits" is a risky scenario. Some things are better off when you don't mess with them, like friendships and rattlesnakes.

Always chase after your dreams.
Unless those dreams get a restraining
order. In that case, you need to leave
your fucking ex alone.

Sliding into DMs is so passive; show some fucking passion and crawl through a second-story window if you want to get my attention.

Love is often compared to fireworks
because both begin with a spark,
but can easily end with a house fire
when instability is involved.

As kids, we were afraid of monsters
under the bed. As adults, we know
the real terror is waking up in bed
with one you met the night before.

If you don't have fun plans tonight, don't feel bad; lots of other people don't either. You know, like parents, patients, and prisoners.

Everyone will have an opinion about your life, but not everyone will give you good advice. Some would rather see you fuck up instead of rise up.

Forget about fitting a mold that other people have created. Unless you truly want to be a loaf of bread, just be yourself until you're dead.

What you see is what you get. Unless you're super drunk when you meet someone "hot" at a bar. In that case, what you see you might soon regret.

Relax, nobody on Tinder wants to murder you and make you into a skin suit. It's the middle of summer; it's too hot for that kind of outfit.

Relationship Goal: Meet a sexy stranger on airplane. Then, the airplane fucking crashes and we die before we have time to get bored of each other.

So, besides drinking wine, sleeping, and liking cute animal memes, do you have any actual hobbies?

I'm not a religious man, but I just walked past some guys vaping while talking about gluten allergies. If that's Hell, count me fucking out.

Dating someone in hopes of changing
them is like ordering water expecting
it to become wine: Both require
miracles that you likely can't perform.

I want a girl with sharp fingernails, but a blunt sense of humor. You know, the kind of girl who can cut you with her hands AND her sarcasm.

Stress is good for you; it helps you discover what you're capable of. Like, how loud can you yell? Or, how many drinks is actually too many?

Every day you wake up is a blessing.
Unless you wake up in the back of a
strange van. That would fucking suck.

Be careful with a girl who wears leggings as both casual and formal wear; she's comfortable in ANY situation — including a murder investigation.

Everything happens for a reason.
Sometimes that reason is because
you're too narcissistic to admit you're
the problem and not the universe.

If you want to impress her, don't just open the door, try opening a fucking book sometime so you can talk about something other than sports.

Going to a bar alone isn't weird. What's weird is going to a bar expecting to meet your soulmate when you literally can't even see straight.

"Intimidating" is a compliment. Any guy who tries to use that as a diss, probably goes home and Googles sad shit like, "How to French kiss."

It's sad when a pet is dressed better than its owner. Like, "Your dog looks fly, Ashley — we can't say the same about your outfit though."

Stop beating yourself up every time
you make the same dumb mistakes
when you drink. Take that as a sign and
embrace the monster you've become.

History allows you to learn from those before you. Who knows, in 100 years, people might study your life to avoid making the same mistakes.

If you're going to fall in love with something, fall in love with yourself. Even though you're a fucking mess.

Even the most beautiful pottery
began as a pile of mud. So, if you're a
fucking mess, be like mud — at least
be a fucking mess with potential.

Why do so many guys act like the friend zone is so terrible? Dude, YOU HAVE A FRIEND, stop fucking complaining and go see a movie together.

Don't change to be accepted. If you're weird, be weird. If you're a nerd, be a nerd. If you're hungry, don't pretend you "just ate."

It's known as "catcalling" because neither cats nor women want to be bothered. You have to earn their attention and affection, you fucking bum.

No matter what you do, some people are going to hate you. So, do what you want, be weird as fuck — give them good reason to think that you suck.

Sharks don't fucking care if they make others uncomfortable. Sharks just swim through life, doing their thing, chasing after shit they want.

I've decided dinner, drinks, and a movie by myself is my new favorite thing. It's like going on a date, but nobody goes home disappointed.

Girls love cheap wine because they like things that are bottled-up and bitter — like their emotions.

When choosing between dating two people, always choose the one with a better sense of humor. Because they'll need it to deal with your shit.

It's called "falling" in love
because falling down is fucking
embarrassing and makes you
look like a clumsy idiot.

One could say I'm an expert in risk management, as in, I always manage to put myself in risky situations. It's how I prefer to live.

Before you go out this weekend, think to yourself, "Do I have money for this?" Then, immediately start brainstorming ways to get free drinks.

Don't introduce yourself by buying someone a drink; introduce yourself by spilling a drink on them. Set proper expectations from the get-go.

A girl's life can change in the blink of an eye. One bad blink and her fake eyelashes are gone, revealing herself as a mere mortal.

Dating is like falling in love with a
song on the radio — then committing
to the entire album — hoping the rest
of the songs aren't fucking garbage.

There's an exception to everything,
except dumbing yourself down or
not being the real you to impress
somebody. That will always be stupid.

Always prepare. Think before you speak, eat before you drink, bathe before you bang, and take a deep breath before you send that risky text.

I want a girl with goals and a good imagination. Like, she has a real job, but she could easily get paid for the weird shit she does in bed.

Girls with houseplants make good girlfriends. Because they've learned to care for something that just sits around all day being fucking useless.

The uncertainty of going to a bar is what makes it fun: Maybe you get bored and go home early, maybe you wake up and fucking hate yourself.

NATIONAL ROLLERCOASTER DAY

Finally, a holiday to celebrate your
emotional instability.

Dating is like being stranded at sea: There's water everywhere, but you're going to die alone because it's all toxic, bitter, and disgusting.

If you refresh your notifications more than three times in a row, your account should lock until you submit video proof of yourself engaging with another human.

Your past does not define you; life
is designed to change you. Friends,
hobbies, haircuts — they all change
(thank God). Change with them.

When one door closes, another opens.
But if you're going to take your drink
outside, please use a plastic cup.

Always take advice from someone with black lipstick. Because they're probably a witch, and fixing your dumb ass is going to require magic.

You know what's sexy? Not being a bitch. You know what's even sexier? Being a bitch. This is why dating is so confusing.

I respect people who refer to their
dog as their "child." It takes courage
to admit you'll never find someone
to have an actual kid with.

Perfection doesn't exist. So if you're going to be a perfectionist, be a drunk perfectionist and stress less with lower standards of perfection.

Don't refer to your relationship
as "on and off," refer to it as
"spontaneous." That makes it sound
fun, instead of fucking ridiculous.

You don't need a "happily ever after,"
you need someone who makes
you realize what matters. And that
person will be a pain in the ass.

What kind of sick fuck wants to be a dentist? Seriously, mouths are fucking gross; people put fucking dicks in there.

I want a girl who's bossy, but not a total bitch. Like, she'll tell me to go fuck myself for no reason, but always says, "Please."

It's not what you say, it's what you portray. I mean, you can say, "No thanks," but it's pretty damn obvious you want some of my fries.

The people you date are like the movies you watch: If they're not worth recommending to a friend, they're not worth seeing again.

I once spent 30 minutes arguing with someone about Bigfoot. Easily on my Top 10 list of "Best Conversations I've Had with a Stranger at a Bar."

I want to date a girl who's like a tiger:
A beautiful creature with nice hair,
but also kind of scary and definitely
capable of killing me.

Honesty is always the best policy.
Unless you like cats, kale, or being
peed on during sex — you should
definitely lie about that shit.

Don't hate Monday, be Monday: Not liked by everyone, but important to a few. And never change. No matter how many people talk shit about you.

Smell is the most memorable sense. In other words, you should worry more about your armpits than your abs and your breath more than your breasts.

Being stuck in a lame conversation
is the intellectual equivalent of being
stuck in traffic. Be grateful you're not
driving and can legally drink.

Don't be cocky. Just as easily as she can match six weird items into a stylish outfit, she can find six other dudes who would be a good fit.

If a relationship is less about
connection and more about
convenience, stay single and enjoy
a constantly-winging-it style of
independence.

It's called a birthday because you're only supposed to celebrate for A DAY. Not a week, not a month, and definitely not with a fucking tiara.

It's going to be really weird when history books begin documenting events with screenshots instead of illustrations and photography.

Depressing thoughts fuel desperate texts. Stop thinking you're going to die alone, put down your phone, and go outside before you text your ex.

Breakfast food is like sex: It's good any time of the day, it's all you think about when you're drunk, and of course, it's best when it's free.

Stop acting insecure; she's not thinking
about other men during sex. In fact,
she's not even thinking about sex, she's
wondering what to watch next on Netflix.

Have you ever woken up from a
sex dream and still felt horny?
Cool, that's pretty much how your
girlfriend feels after real sex.

I want a girl who's not picky, but very protective. Like, she'll eat anywhere, but if you touch her fry basket, she'll put you in a casket.

Everybody's a good person. That is, until you start looking for matches on a dating app and become so judgmental that you begin to hate even yourself.

Dating is like grocery shopping: You know what you should be looking for, but all bets are off when you see something delicious and bad for you.

When you sneeze, that's your soul trying to leave your body. Probably because it's embarrassed by all the dumb shit you're thinking about.

Girls love fancy, multi-flavored
Frappuccinos because those drinks
are exactly like them: sweet, cold,
and fucking complicated.

Your grandpa used to write your
grandma love letters longer than a
college thesis. Now, here you are,
texting women pictures of your penis.

Monday is society's way of reminding you that — despite your best weekend efforts — you're not actually a rapper, rockstar, or real housewife.

If someone at a bar doesn't think you're attractive, it's not your fault; it's theirs because they didn't drink enough to make you look good.

I just want a home with a moat. A home that says, "Don't bother me, but stay on my good side because I might have a pool party next weekend."

Whenever you obsess over dumb things you've done, know that you're not alone; your mom also wonders why you constantly make bad decisions.

If she can throw a fit, she can row a boat. In other words, be glad she only yells at your mistakes, instead of dumping your body in a lake.

I want a girl who's crazy, but considerate. Like, if she stays home on a Friday night, she's not resting, she's giving the world a break.

Dating is like driving a car: We all kind of suck at it, but we're trying our best not to kill anyone.

I'm fine going to Hell; becoming a guardian angel sounds like a hassle. You mean to tell me I just died and now I have to babysit? Fuck that.

Stop second-guessing; start seriously trusting. Obey your instincts, say what you're thinking — be as confident as you are while drinking.

Forcing a relationship is like
walking a dog that can't be tamed:
You're tethered together, but both
pretty miserable.

Guys, a nice car is cool — but unless
you're also an interesting person —
a road trip with you would feel more
like a fucking kidnapping.

Developing a crush is similar to getting a bee sting: It's quick, unexpected, and painfully annoying when you're just trying to have a good time.

I'm convinced that anyone who sleeps comfortably on an airplane can also comfortably kill another human being. Serial killers wear neck pillows.

In life, be a fucking burrito: Always leave people wanting more, but at the same time, kind of regretful about how much they've already had.

If a group of crows is called a murder, an all-girl group text should be called a slaughter. Because that's exactly what happens to your screenshots.

Why do bugs always have sex in gross places? You have wings — YOU CAN LITERALLY FLY ANYWHERE — take her somewhere romantic, you fucking bum.

The Bachelor is a pretty accurate series. That "nice guy" you're falling for, is probably saying the same shit to at least eight other women.

Making breakfast won't make you
"wifey material." Eggs are so easy.
Build a career, respect yourself, bake
a fucking cake — then we'll talk.

If you're tempted to text your ex, plug your nose and hold your breath. If you're lucky, you'll pass out before sending that dumb text out.

Get yourself a girl who keeps your business as secretive to others as she does the list of baby names she's been curating since junior high.

We don't need a border wall. We need a wall to separate people who don't text back from the rest of us trying to live in a civilized world.

Good manners are important. Open doors, say "thank you," and ALWAYS tell your dog he's a good boy. (Seriously, he puts up with so much shit.)

I want a girl who loves to travel, but also likes staying in. You know, the kind of girl who will visit me if I end up in a foreign prison.

A sloth is basically the creature
everyone aspires to be on a Sunday:
no fucks, no makeup, just chowing
down and hanging around.

She's got a face like the Sun, but a soul like an eclipse. Basically, she's pretty, but kind of a bitch.

Halloween is the one day you're
encouraged to be fucking creepy, weird,
or gross, and what do you do? Dress up
and pretend to be somebody else.

Good grammar is fucking attractive. If you know how to properly use a comma, there's a good chance I'm going to want to get on ya.

Love is just a word; commitment
is an action. I mean, most people
claim to love their bed, but can't
even commit to a fucking bedtime.

Guys, if she punctuates her texts, be careful. She's not afraid to put an end to things. Like run-on sentences, a relationship, or your life.

After a political race, it's nice to see regular commercials on TV again. "I don't even have a yard, but that leaf blower looks fucking great."

I want a girl with common sense, but uncommon style. Like, she can solve just about anything, but every day she dresses like it's Halloween.

Life is a fucking circus and we're all
just trying to find someone capable
of juggling our bullshit.

You shouldn't even bother dressing up on Halloween — you've been ghosting girls all year — just keep being your worthless, spooky self.

You can't go out dressed as a
sexy dog or cute cat and call it a
"Halloween costume" — you've been
that creature all year on Snapchat.

You know that nervous feeling you get when you really want to impress someone? Ignore that, be yourself — even though you're pretty annoying.

Stop apologizing for things that
you're clearly not going to stop doing.
Overreacting, drunk texting, being
annoying — that's you, own it.

You need a guide dog, but not because you're blind, just a dog that walks you home from the bar and into your bed when you're being a drunk idiot.

Girls, if you want to test your
relationship, dress REALLY fucking scary
for Halloween and see how awkward he
gets around you: Wear a wedding dress.

Enjoy suffering alone with a hangover.
Some people are less fortunate; they
have hangovers AND responsibilities.
They're called "parents."

Ladies, if he's distant, suspicious, and unreliable — you don't have a boyfriend — you have a fucking cat.

I want a girl who's responsible, but irrational. Like, she always makes her car payment on time, but she used that car to run over her ex.

HALLOWEEN

Halloween parties are the best parties
because there's no bigotry, only
acceptance. A mummy playing beer pong
with a baby? Nobody fucking cares.

Adjusting to life after Halloween
is kind of depressing, like leaving
Hogwarts: No more wizards, no more
witches, just bros and basic bitches.

True friends will always stick around,
even when you're crying. If you
have these, consider yourself lucky.
Because crying is fucking gross.

If you have time for drama, you have time for a second job. Stop gossiping and go make milkshakes instead of talking about others' mistakes.

If you can't commit to plans, at least commit to an excuse. Don't just tell me your phone died — flake the fuck out and fake your own death.

Don't fear rejection; fear responsibility. If you approach that person, they WILL fall in love with you. And that's now your fault.

Dudes, trim your fingernails. Your girl just spent 25 minutes shaving her legs; the least you can do is not claw at them like a fucking goblin.

Girls, stay safe tonight. Statistically, three percent of men are psychopaths. These men will fucking kill you. They are known to say, "I'm not like other guys."

Dating is the way it is because the "floor is lava" game taught us all to avoid obvious stability and jump onto something unbalanced instead.

The cool thing about opinions is the fact that you don't have to listen to them. Like a terrible song, just tune them out and keep moving along.

Your opinion is music to my ears,
but it's like hearing "Despacito"
on repeat for 26 minutes.

Every "wyd" text should receive an "l-o-l" response. Because it's fucking comical to think you're too cool to ask her out using actual words.

Trying to figure out why a girl is
mad is like trying to figure out why
headphones get so tangled: Give up.
It just happens.

Dating is like eating a fruit salad:
In the beginning, it's full of options —
but eventually — all that's left is
tasteless leftover honeydew.

If you don't drink, but you're curious
what a hangover feels like, it's
basically just a mix of starvation,
confusion, and life evaluation.

Stop whining. Maybe she keeps taking
your hoodies because she's making
you a gift that requires measurements.
Like a sweater — or a coffin.

Enjoy yourself tonight, but wear protection. And by that, I mean, wear a helmet with those heels. They look good, but you're kinda clumsy.

Don't get cocky. If she can ignore the pain of fashionable shoes, she can definitely ignore your texts if you start acting too fucking cool.

The worst thing to be in life is anything other than yourself. Be real, be authentic — fuck being fake or generic. Or racist. Fuck that too.

Don't hide your emotions — let your tears create fear — remind him how easily you can fake cry to cops investigating a suspicious disappearance.

In life, there comes a point when you need to stop thinking and just start acting. For most of us, that's somewhere between drinks six and seven.

What's cooler than canceled plans? Keeping your word. Be there, be reliable — be the one who's always on time and already three drinks ahead.

Believing in yourself is refusing to admit
you're wrong because deep down you
know you're surrounded by idiots.

Your phone is more powerful than the Moon-landing computers. So, I don't know, maybe use it for more than just insecure internet stalking.

THANKSGIVING

If you're single and you live alone, you
should enjoy being lonely. Be thankful,
stop whining, and appreciate the silence
of not having roommates or kids.

Uber and Tinder are basically the same thing: You agree to meet a stranger, hoping they take you home and you don't die.

News anchors have the worst jokes.
It's like getting weather and traffic
updates from a box of popsicle sticks.

I'm going to tell my kids they can be anything they want in life. Except a DJ, a mermaid, or a terrorist. We already have too many of those.

Dating is like picking boogers: Pick carefully, because some people will stick around no matter how hard you try to flick them away.

The best part of having a college degree:
You don't have to post photos trying to
sell some bullshit Instagram skinny tea.

I want a girl with bright eyes, but a dark soul. Like, you're mesmerized when you talk to her, but at the same time, you're afraid you might fucking die.

If someone doesn't appreciate you,
don't get mad, get gone; leave them
hanging. While you're out drinking
drinks, petting pups — living life.

It's crazy how focused you can suddenly become while drunk. One minute, you're a fucking disaster; the next, you have no purpose other than food, sex, or a bed.

Overthinking almost always leads to underperforming. So, get after it, make a move, and wear that outfit even though others disapprove.

If her eyeliner is flawless, always be honest. Because she'll draw the line and cut through your bullshit with the same skillful precision.

There's a big difference between seeking advice and seeking attention. For starters, if it's a social media plea, they're usually just saying, "Look at me."

I don't believe the apple story because anyone with Satan's experience would have known to tempt Eve using a puppy and not a fucking snake.

Aliens are probably watching us decorate the corpses of dead trees for Christmas like, "Damn, those are some sick fucks. Let's skip this planet."

I like winter because it gets dark early.
So you don't feel like a piece of shit
getting drunk at 4 P.M.

If you sleep with an ex in December, it's okay. Call it a visit from the Ghost of Christmas Past and consider it a valuable holiday lesson.

Celebrities give their children weird names because they don't want their kids to grow up to become boring and basic. Like you, David.

Good luck finding the perfect I-like-you-but-I'm-confused-about-where-this-is-going gift for whomever you're "dating" this holiday season.

Girls, the next time a guy sends you
a dick pic, save the photo, put a filter
on it, and send it back saying,
"Here, I tried to fix it."

A life with no regrets is a life with no reflection. And, you need reflection. To not only fix your hellish hair, but also your selfish life.

You can't say, "as black as my soul," then cry every time you see a dog adoption commercial. Make up your mind, are you fucking evil or not?

Find someone who's as protective
of you as they are with their phone
when somebody else is holding it and
scrolling through their pictures.

Every good weekend has three
different stories: your story, your
friend's story, and the story you tell
your boss in order to keep your job.

I want a girl who cares about her health, but not her sobriety. Like, she does yoga, but her water bottle is usually full of vodka.

Oh, you're tired and don't like Monday?
What happened to all that "I'll sleep
when I'm dead" talk you were shouting
at the bar last weekend?

Instead of autocorrecting "yas" or "bae," your phone should just autodial a local therapist to get you some fucking help.

If she only wears black, be careful;
she's either a witch or a supervillain.
Makes for fun dating, but she'll end
your life without hesitating.

There are 206 bones in the human body and none of them are located in your heart. In other words, your heart can't be broken; stop whining.

Marriage is like finding the prize inside a box of cereal: You have to dig through a lot of shit to find someone, and when you do, it isn't even that great.

If you're easily offended, your feelings are like snowflakes: Fragile and annoying, but I kind of enjoy hearing them crunch beneath my feet.

Going home for the holidays helps you realize that the greatest gifts in life are often the ones you give yourself, like the gift of moving.

This Christmas, remember there are people less fortunate than you: people who can't sleep diagonal, people who have to share a bed . . . people who are married.

If getting the "perfect body" is your resolution (yet again), pick a different goal. Better yet, just pick up a fucking book and read something.

I want a girl with a clean house, but a filthy mind. Like, her bedroom is well-kept, but the shit she does in there would upset her parents.

Heavy winter coats suck. If I enjoyed feeling weighed down, I'd move back to my hometown and hang out with everyone I knew in high school.

Dogs will never realize how popular and loved they are by society. No dog is ever going to read this book; that sucks.

Talking with coworkers after the holidays is like a bad first date: You don't care what the person is saying, but be nice and pretend you do.

Stop trying to change yourself every year with new resolutions; just accept the fact that you're a fucking mess.

ABOUT THE AUTHOR

Writer. Creator. Instigator. Not your dad.

@SGRSTK

45981756R00208

Printed in Poland
by Amazon Fulfillment
Poland Sp. z o.o., Wrocław